Message of Bhagavad Gita

(In 126 Chosen Shlokas)

Part 2: TAT - Glory of the Lord

Transcribed and Edited by Atmajyotis
(Based on Sri Prabhuji's Satsangs)

An offering from

LIGHT OF THE SELF FOUNDATION

Dedication

Many Atmajyotis have worked selflessly to transcribe
and publish this book based on talks of
Sadguru Sri Prabhuji.

With deep love and respect we dedicate this book to
all Atmajyotis. May this effort of all Atmajyotis reach
spiritual seekers all over the world, with this intention,
we release this book.

lokāha samasthāha sukhino bhavantu

Gita Jayanthi, December 2022

TABLE OF CONTENTS

FOREWORD

Srimad Bhagavad Gita is the sacred teaching of Sri Krishna. During the Kurukshetra war, Arjuna's mind was full of anxiety and sorrow; he was confused between Dharma and *adharma*. Bhagavad Gita is the teaching of Sri Krishna to the confused and depressed Arjuna. He was shown the path ofDharma by the supreme grace of the Lord.

Bhagavad Gita however isn't just a message delivered to Arjuna alone, it is the universal message given by the Vishwa Guru Sri Krishna to the entire human race. Arjuna was just an instrument. It is a sacred teaching for each and every one of us. What is the teaching? The Gita gives us the wisdom to attain liberation. It is a sacred scripture that shows us the path to mukti and uplifts us.

What do we have to do for that? ***ātmano mokshārtam jagad hitayacha*** - (Self Realization and service for the world) should be the mantra of our life. Hence the main teaching of Sri Krishna in Bhagavad Gita is *Brahma Vidya* (Knowledge of the Absolute) and *Yoga Shastra* (Yogic Science). Once we realize that the individual self and the supreme Self are one and the same, we attain moksha, we are liberated. Hence Sri Krishna teaches the truth of the inner self through Brahma Vidya, the knowledge that helps us merge with the supreme Self, Paramātma. To attain this knowledge, Brahmajnāna, the mind should be purified. Hence Sri Krishna teaches us Yoga Shastra - how to lead an ethical and moral life and walk on the path ofDharma. This alone helps us to purify our minds.

yatra yogeśhvaraḥ kṛiṣhṇo
yatra pārtho dhanur-dharaḥ
tatra Srir vijayo bhūtir
dhruvā nītir matir mama

Wherever there is Sri Krishna, the Lord of all Yoga, and wherever there is Arjuna, the supreme archer, there will also certainly be unending opulence, victory, prosperity, and righteousness. Of this, I am certain.

This sloka highlights the supreme importance of studying the Gita. Just like Arjuna, we should all become disciples of Sri Krishna. The teaching of Gita should be implemented in our day-to-day life. Only then 'Sri', meaning success in material life and 'Vijaya', meaning success in spiritual life will be obtained. This is the most important verse told by Sri Krishna in the last verse of the last chapter of the Bhagavad Gita (BG 18.78). The ones who study and implement Bhagavad Gita in their day-to-day life and teach this supreme knowledge to others are the closest and most lovable to God. Is there anything more important in life than being close to God?

Atmajyoti Satsang's Gita Jyoti Study Circles have many volunteers who are doing selfless service. The acharyas and acharyanis of the Study Circles are involved in various activities like teaching Bhagavad Gita verses, explaining their meaning, giving discourses, and generally spreading the message of the Gita to the world. They are an inspiration to many people. This seva is sure to bring a lot of good merit to all, because this activity is most lovable to God.

With the intention of passing the message of Bhagavad Gita in a simplified manner, 126 slokas from the 18 chapters have been carefully selected and summarized into a book. There are many Atmajyotis who have put in efforts to preserve my teachings and transcribe them into a book which is understandable to one and all. May the Supreme Lord bless them and their families. May their efforts be fruitful. May the light and wisdom of Gita flow into the lives of many more and uplift the entire world.

Sri Prabhuji

December 2022

PREFACE

The Bhagavad Gita is the song sung by the Lord. Listening to the Bhagavad Gita, chanting its verses and spreading the knowledge of Bhagavad Gita is considered very noble work.

Of all the *yajnas* and *pujas* that we offer to the Almighty, offering or spreading the wisdom of the scriptures is the greatest and noblest of all. All forms of worship give us good merit, but the greatest merit is gained by *jnāna yajna*, the service of spreading the Lord's message to the world.

Bhagavad Gita is a spiritual scripture. The path of spirituality shows us the divinity within. We look for God everywhere; we go to temples and undertake pilgrimage. But salvation lies only in realizing our own divinity. Bhagavad Gita is the Song of the Lord Himself, the ultimate truth imparted by Bhagavān Sri Krishna to Arjuna. Thus one who wishes to reach the ultimate reality has to necessarily study the Gita.

The Gita is the essence of all our scriptures - the Upanishads and the Vedas. Vedas are four in number - *Rigveda, Yajurveda, Sāmaveda and Atharvana Veda*. They begin with *karmakānda* and end with *jnānakānda*. In the *jnānakānda*, the portion which explains the meaning and essence of Vedas is called Upanishad. Upanishad consists of the essence of all the Vedas. There are several Upanishads, 108 or even more. Out of these, the three great acharyas - Shankara, Madhva and Ramanuja have written the abstract or bhashya for ten important Upanishads.

The Upanishads contain the revelations of our ancient sages about the truth of existence - which is 'I am in the divine and the divine is in me'. The study of the Upanishads is also a *jnāna yajna*. The essence of the Upanishads is narrated by Sri Krishna to Arjuna in the Bhagavad Gita. Therefore if we study the Gita, the truth realized by the great rishis will be realized by us as well.

The realization of this Truth is called Jnāna. Jnāna destroys *ajnāna* - that about which we are ignorant. What is it that we do not know? We know everything about the outer world, like how to be a businessman, an engineer, how to cook etc. But what we do not know is, 'Who am I?' We assume that 'I' refers to the body, man or woman. We can go only as far as the body, mind and intellect and we think this is 'I'.

The Bhagavad Gita eliminates this ignorance about our identity with body, mind and intellect. It reveals that they are only the instruments or vehicles through which we operate!

Says Bhagavān, your mind, body and intellect are also vehicles, just as a car, bus or airplane is. You are the passenger, the *jivātma* who inhabits the body, mind and intellect. You are the Paramātma, the energy driving this vehicle. *mukti* or liberation is when you, the *jiva* realizes 'I am not this body, mind and intellect, I am one in the divine, I am *ātmaswaroopi*. So the essence of Bhagavad Gita is,

**nānu, nānembudu nānalla
ee deha mana buddhi nānalla
sachchidānandātma shiva nānu nāne
shivoham shivoham shivoham**

I am not what I think I am, I am not this body and mind or intellect; I am pure consciousness, Shivoham, Shivoham, Shivoham.

Over several lifetimes, we would've experienced a lot of good and bad things, accumulated merits and demerits. To experience and exhaust the results of these good-bad results, we have to be reborn yet again and again, *punarapi maranam, punarapi jananam, punarapi janani jatare shayanam,* sings Adi Shankaracharya; we are compelled to go through the repeated cycles of birth and death, and thus we end up in the mother's womb again and again.

With every new birth comes ajnāna, ignorance. With ignorance comes *pāpa-punya*, merit and demerit, which keep accumulating. This treasure-chest of endless *pāpa-punya* can be emptied only by diving into the *jnāna* of Bhagavad Gita.

"Can I let only the demerits go, and hang on to the merits?" is the clever question asked by the mind! But, says Krishna, both *pāpa-punya*, good-bad should go, because both are shackles that bind us. pāpa is the iron shackle and punya is the golden shackle, and we do not know which one binds us in what manner, both will certainly bind us to birth and death. Releasing ourselves from this bondage by realizing that "I am divine' is the message of Bhagavad Gita.

Right now, we operate in the world assuming, boasting that 'I am everything! There is no God! I am God!' The exact opposite of this is Self Realization - 'God is everything, There is nothing called I, I implies the ego'. When this realization happens, this is called *ātma jnāna, advaita jnāna.* We should study Bhagavad Gita for this advaita jnāna, the knowledge of liberation. There are 18 chapters in the Bhagavad Gita. It can be classified into three groups of six chapters each. In the first six chapters, the Lord explains who we are. In the next 6 chapters, He reveals about Himself, that is Ishwara, the creator. In the last 6 chapters, that is from 13th to 18th chapters, He explains about our relationship with God. Thus the

Bhagavad Gita is the essence of the *mahavākya* of Upanishads - *tat tvam asi* - That Thou Art.

tat means 'Ishwara', **tvam** means 'you', **asi** means 'you are Ishwara', which means you are the form of Ishwara. We may feel "oh no, how is this possible? how can I be the form of God, this is not acceptable, this is thought is sin, this is injustice". This happens because we mistake the I for the Ego. When we stop identifying with the Ego, the real 'I' is revealed, we will realize 'I am Ishwara'. That is liberation, taught in the Bhagavad Gita.

ātma darshanam brahma darshanam
brahma darshanam satya darshanam

First and foremost we need to investigate, understand and become aware of what or who is this 'I'. This is called *ātma darshana*. Once we are aware about who we are, then the awareness of God will happen. This is called *brahma darshana*. Realizing that *ātma* and *brahma* are the same is *satya darshana*. This is the ultimate truth and everything else is a lie, a dream, an illusion - *māya*. The Bhagavad Gita leads us out of this illusion.

So, what is the subject matter of the Bhagavad Gita? Essentially, the Gita talks about two things - Jnāna (wisdom) and Karma (action). What kind of *jnāna*?

ātmajnāna; who am I, what is my relationship with God? What is Karma? How to lead life, how to perform action, how to purify my heart and attain liberation - this is called Karma-marga, the Path of Karma. *atmajnāna* implies *brahmajnāna*. Karma tells the way to lead our life. Understand these two and you will be liberated, says Lord Krishna.

No other scripture in the entire world teaches the means of liberation with such clarity and simplicity. The Gita has more than 700 verses. It might not be possible for most of us to study all the 700-plus verses; hence this effort of distilling the essence of the Bhagavad Gita in 126 selected verses. The summary of these 126 verses have been further divided into three parts and published as three separate books; hence we need to read all the three books to get the entire essence of the Gita.

This book has the summary of chapters 7 to 12, explained with the selected verses, and published as SECRETS OF BHAGAVAD GITA Part 2: TAT - Glory of the Lord.

- Sri Prabhuji

CHAPTER 7: JNĀNA VIJNĀNA YOGA

Summary

My Pranāms to all the Atmajyotis, Divine Light of the Self.

Knowledge is of two kinds. What we get through the sense organs and the mind is called 'indirect knowledge' or *jnāna* because it is filtered through them. For whom is it indirect? For the Self or *ātma* or *sākshi* it is indirect knowledge. The Witness or *sākshi* can also give us experiential knowledge directly through awareness. This process does not involve the senses or mind. Therefore it is called 'direct knowledge' or *vijnāna*.

We can also look at this from another angle. Direct experience of the Self by the Self is *vijnāna.* The seventh chapter of the Bhagavad Gita deals with *jnāna and vijnāna.* Sri Krishna is describing his own divine nature. He is always aware that he is the Supreme Reality. The cosmos is also an expression of his Being. Therefore whatever he describes is vijnāna or Direct Knowledge to him. To Arjuna who has not yet realized his true nature and is filtering the information through his senses and intellect, this is jnāna or Indirect Knowledge.

Shloka 7.3

Amongst thousands of persons, hardly one strives for perfection; and amongst those who have achieved perfection, hardly one knows Me in truth

manuṣhyāṇāṁ sahasreṣhu - among thousands of human beings, *kaśhchid yatati siddhaye* - only some people make an effort; *yatatām api siddhānāṁ* - of those who make the effort, *kaśhchin māṁ vetti tattvataḥ* - only a few realize Me in my essence.

Like everything in life, there will be quite a few people who will be putting in a lot of effort, but out of all these only a few people become successful. For example, about 10 lakh (one million) students join primary school in one state for education. But those who join high school are only four lakh which means six lakh children drop out of school by the time they come to high school. Out of the four lakh children who joined high school, only two lakh students join college. Of these two lakh students, there can be approximately 50,000 joining Engineering colleges and approximately two hundred to 300 students enroll for PhD. This is due to the natural elimination process which happens in life. Not everyone who tries, gets what they need. This can be due to lack of ability, intensity, faith and focus required to reach the final goal.

It is the same in businesses also. There are millions of businessmen in the world and everyone wants to make money. But only some people become highly successful and out of these, there are only a handful of people who become billionaires. Not every businessman turns into a billionaire.

This is exactly the same thing in spiritual life also. There are millions and billions of people on this planet and not everyone is interested in the spiritual truth or in realizing God. There are many people who want to realize God and they put in a certain amount of effort but quite a few lack the required faith, intensity and focus because of which they drop out from their spiritual journey. Only a handful of them make it to the final to realize the divinity within them. Only a handful realize the divine form of *atma* in them. Bhagavān says that such people are rare, but it is not that it is due to some sort of discrimination in this universe. Bhagavān never discriminates between people. These people are rare because only a handful of people put in efforts, faith and intense efforts to realize God.

For realizing God, we need to put consistent efforts and be very focused. We need to take the inward journey for realizing God through the help of Karma Yoga, Bhakti Yoga, Jnāna Yoga and Kriyā Yoga. We need to start our inward journey which should be consistent. This will ultimately lead to success and we will realize the Supreme Lord in us. This is the most blissful experience anyone can have and it is called *brāhmi sthiti*. It is the peak of human achievement, but how many people are ready for that?

For many, God is not the end. God is just the means. People do meditation and prayer to get some benefit out of God but not necessarily get God himself. There is a beautiful story to illustrate this. Once Goddess Lakshmi, the Goddess of Wealth was having a discussion with Lord Narayana, the Supreme Lord. Said Lakshmi, "More people are after me", which Lord Narayana denied, "No. More people are after me". Goddess Lakshmi smiled and suggested that they put people to test. Lord Narayana agreed, went down to earth in the form of a poor Brahmin and visited the King in his palace. There he recited the Vedas. Pleased, the king requested the Brahmin to stay close to him, and made arrangements for him to stay in a palace adjacent to the King's, with all the required facilities.

After a couple of days, Goddess Lakshmi, resplendent and bejeweled, came down in a golden chariot and proceeded towards the palace. People on the street were mesmerized by the dazzling gold, and the King rushed to the palace door to welcome her and offered her food and drink. Whatever she touched turned into gold and the king was stunned. At once, he fell at her feet and requested her to stay in his palace. "Ok" said Lakshmi, "but where is the place for me to stay here?" The King replied immediately, "Oh, there is a palace next door just for you!", and before the Brahmin could realize what hit him, he was thrown out of the palace to accommodate Goddess Lakshmi.

So, though most people strive for God, it is not for God himself but for some benefit from God. There are very few people who really strive for realizing God in their heart and only these people will become successful.

manuṣhyāṇāṁ sahasreṣhu
kaśhchid yatati siddhaye I
yatatām api siddhānāṁ
kaśhchin māṁ vetti tattvataḥ II 7.3 II

****

Shloka 7.4

Earth, water, fire, air, space, mind, intellect, and ego—these are eight components of My material energy

There are two types of nature - *prakriti* - of Bhagavān; *bhūmir-āpo 'nalo vāyuḥ khaṁ* - the five elements of earth, water, fire, wind, space, and *mana buddhir eva cha* - mind, intellect and ahankara, ego. These are the eight fold nature of Bhagavān, His lower nature.

Look at ourselves, we have a body, we have a mind, we have an intellect, we have an ego and we have consciousness. The body is made up of five elements, earth element, water element, fire element, wind element and space element. Then we have mind, intellect and ego. We are nothing but a miniature replica of the universe. Universe is consisting of space, wind, fire, water and earth elements. These form the basic raw material for the entire creation. The whole of the creation consisting of stars, planets, galaxies is made up of these five elements only and beyond these five elements there is mind, intellect and ego at the universal level. So these are the eight aspects of the lower nature of Bhagavān. Just like we have a gross body consisting of earth element and all the other four elements, the Lord has a gross body which is this universe. There is a similarity between what is there in the individual and what is there in the universal, except that the universal is on a larger scale. So Lord explains his lower form of nature. Then he goes on to explain his higher form of nature, which we will see in the next shloka.

bhūmir-āpo 'nalo vāyuḥ
khaṁ mano buddhir eva cha I
ahankāra itīyaṁ me
bhinnā prakṛitir aṣhṭadhā II 7.4 II

****

Shloka 7.5

Such is My inferior energy. But beyond it, O mighty-armed Arjuna, I have a superior energy. This is the jīva śhakti (the soul energy), which comprises the embodied souls who are the basis of life in this world

So Bhagavān outlined his lower nature consisting of five elements, mind, intellect and ego. Beyond this there is higher nature which is actually chetana or consciousness. Again this is something similar to how an individual is. An individual is a miniature replica of the universe - we have a body made up of five elements, we have mind, we have intellect and we have consciousness.

Consciousness is our higher nature. Consciousness is the source of all the powers of the body. Similarly the conscious nature of Bhagwan is the source of all the power in the universe. Conscious nature, Consciousness, is the higher nature of the Lord. The lower nature consists of five elements, the mind, intellect and ego, the higher nature consists of consciousness. To know the Lord in totality (God Realization) is to know the entire nature of the Lord. This is the purpose of Sri Krishna outlining his nature.

apareyam itas tvanyāṁ
prakṛitiṁ viddhi me parām I
jīva-bhūtāṁ mahā-bāho
yayedaṁ dhāryate jagat II 7.5 II

****

Shloka 7.7

There is nothing higher than Myself, O Arjuna. Everything rests in Me, as beads strung on a thread

mattaḥ parataraṁ nānya - there is nothing beyond me; *kiñchid asti dhanañjaya* - O' Dhananjaya, there is nothing beyond me; *mayi sarvam idaṁ protaṁ* - all this what you can see, *sūtre maṇi-gaṇā iva* - are like beads strung on a thread, you can see the beads, you cannot see the string.

Sri Krishna Bhagavān gives a beautiful analogy of a necklace consisting of beads. You can see the beads, but you cannot see the thread that holds the beads. Similarly, you can see everything in the universe, they are like beads, but what you cannot see is the Consciousness which is the thread holding this universe. Without the thread of Consciousness there will be no organization, nor will there be structure in the universe. That Consciousness is the Lord, Bhagavān. Bhagavān earlier outlined his lower nature consisting of the five elements which are the mind, intellect and ego and higher nature consisting of Consciousness.

Now a question may arise in the minds of those who are listening, "Oh! Is there something beyond this? Is there something more than this?" So the Lord affirmatively says nothing is beyond the conscious nature. The conscious nature is ultimate, the conscious nature is the foundation of existence, foundation of the universe. Everything is held by this conscious nature of the Lord.

mattaḥ parataraṁ nānyat

kiñchid asti dhanañjaya I
mayisarvam idaṁ protaṁ
sūtre maṇi-gaṇāiva II 7.7 II

****

Shloka 7.14

This divine energy of Mine, consisting of the three modes of material nature, is difficult to overcome. But those who have surrendered unto Me can easily cross beyond it

māya consists of three gunas; three modes of nature. It's very difficult to cross over but one who depends on me alone, they will be able to cross over. It's very difficult to cross over the *māya*. *māya* is derived from the word *yā-mā*. **yā-mā iti māya.** It means - that which is not there but appears to be there. It appears to be real, very real. The world appears to be very very real. But is it real? When you go to sleep the world disappears from your consciousness and it appears again in the morning. There is constant change in the world. Still the world appears to be solid. So, we attribute reality to the world. We get attracted by objects in the world.

A mirage in the desert is a good example. Somebody passing through a desert sees water on the horizon, gets attracted to it and goes in search of water, to ultimately find that there is no water. Similarly, the world appears to be attractive to us and we keep searching for happiness in the world. There is no happiness in the world, so it is futile to search for it out there. Happiness is our inner nature.

By getting influenced by the three modes of nature called *sattva guna, rajo guna, tamo guna*, people fall into the trap of extracting happiness from the world which is not possible. It is very difficult to cross over this *māya*. The only way is to hold on to the Lord's higher nature, consciousness.

There is a beautiful story about maya in the Vishnu Purana. Narada is a firm and a great devotee of Vishnu. He is very egoistic. He believes that *māya* cannot touch him. Vishnu understands the egoism in Narada and one day while taking a stroll near the seashore, Vishnu tells Narada to get him a glass of water. Narada rushes to the nearest place to get a glass of water. A beautiful lady opens the door. Narada falls in love with her and begs her to marry him. They get married, have children, and Narada forgets all about the glass of water. They have six children and Narada is working in the fields now to earn a livelihood. One day there is a flash flood, and the entire crop is destroyed. The house and the children and the wife of Narada are washed away in the floods. Narada starts wailing and wakes up suddenly - to find Lord Vishnu smiling at him. "Where is my glass of water, Narada?" asks the Lord. In a flash Narada understands the power of *maya* - no one can escape it. When time, space and the world appear, we fall into the trap. Time appears where there is no time. The world appears where there is no space. Such is the power of *maya*.

daivī hyeṣhā guṇa-mayī
mama māya duratyayā I
mām eva ye prapadyante
māyam etāṁ taranti te II 7.14 II

****

Shloka 7.15

Four kinds of people do not surrender unto Me—those ignorant of knowledge, those who lazily follow their lower nature though capable of knowing Me, those with deluded intellect, and those with a demoniac nature

In this verse God speaks of the difficulty in crossing over māya.

māya is the appearance of the universe as reality, a solid reality and it makes us deluded. We forget our own divine nature and start taking the body as the Self which is called *dehātma buddhi*. This is the main contribution of *māya*. We start thinking of ourselves in terms of the body which is of material nature. And this error leads to a lot of wrong actions and corresponding results.

People who take the body to be real are said to have asuri prakruti, demonic nature. There are two types of nature: demonic and divine. While divine nature progressively purifies a human being, demonic nature progressively distorts the thinking and forces one to do evil actions. Demonic nature comes from a wrong understanding of life, wrong understanding of the Self, wrong understanding of myself as the body.

There is a story in an Upanishad. The king of *devatās* Indra and the king of *asurās* Virochana go to Brahmaji to learn about the Self. After serving Brahmaji for many years, Virochana understands Self to be the body and goes back whereas Indra continues for many years serves Brahmaji and then attains the knowledge of Self. Since then demons live with the attitude that the body is the Self. They adore the body, pamper the body and live for the body. So, this is the demonic nature. When you are identified with the body, you become very selfish. All your actions are selfish, and you will collect a lot of impressions in your mind. It is very difficult to get rid of these impressions. That's why those with demonic nature, those who identify themselves with the body, find it very difficult to realize God because He is the innermost core, Consciousness. For those covered in *māya* it is very difficult to go from the outer to inner.

na māṁ duṣhkṛitino mūḍhāḥ
prapadyante narādhamāḥ I
māyayāpahṛita-jnāna
āsuraṁ bhāvam āsritāḥ II 7.15 II

****

Shloka 7.16

O' best amongst the Bharatas, four kinds of pious people engage in My devotion—the distressed, the seekers of knowledge, the seekers of worldly possessions, and those who are situated in knowledge

Four types of people seek the Lord - those who are in difficulty, those who are inquisitive, those who need money and the wise ones, *jnānis*. They pray to the Lord, worship the Lord and constantly move closer to Him. So, they are of four types: *ārtaḥ* - one

28

who is in difficulty. There are people who never think of the Lord when they are in good condition. The moment they land up in any bad situation in life possibly for financial or health or married life they start praying to the Lord to free them from the difficulty. The mind constantly goes to the Lord in a difficult situation. They are the *ārtha*.

Then there is the second category of people - *jijñāsu*. They are inquisitive people. They want to understand what is life, who is God, what is the beginning of the world, what is the cause of the world? They are called *jijñāsuḥ*. The third category of people, *artha-arthī*. They are people who seek wealth, money and power. The fourth category of people who worship the Lord are the wise ones who understand divinity, understand the real nature of Bhagavān - *jñānī*. All four categories of people will eventually attain the Lord. But out of them, the *jñānī* is very close to the Lord because he understands the Lord.

chatur-vidhā bhajante māṁ
janāḥ sukṛitino 'rjuna I
ārto jijñāsur arthārthī
jñānī cha bharataṛṣhabha II 7.16 II

****

Shloka 7.17

Amongst these, I consider those who worship Me with knowledge and are steadfastly and exclusively devoted to Me, to be the highest. I am very dear to them and they are very dear to Me

The *jñānī* is the fourth kind of devotee who has realized his own true nature. He also understands the real nature of the world and God. He knows that the Lord is none other than his inner Self. That is why a jñānī is very close to God.

There is a story in Rāmāyana that illustrates this beautifully. After conquering Lanka, Rama, Sita and Hanuman returned to Ayodhya. Rama was crowned the King of Ayodhya, and Mother Sita was very happy. She wanted to reward Hanuman for his service to Rama. To express her gratitude she gave him her pearl necklace. Hanuman took it and started behaving in a very peculiar manner. He bit through each bead, looked inside, shook his head and threw it away.

Everyone was shocked at his rude behavior. They asked him what he was doing. Hanuman said, "I thought that the pearl necklace that Mother Sita gave me must be very special. So I wanted to see if Rama is present in every pearl. But I was disappointed to see that he is in none of them. Even a necklace made from the most precious gems has no value if Consciousness or Rama is absent." Hearing this everyone marveled at Hanuman's wisdom.

What is the meaning behind this story? What was Hanuman trying to convey? A *jñānī* understands that the nature of the world is illusory. He knows he can get no permanent joy from it. His innermost Self is the *ātma*. *ātma* is one with the *paramātma*. That is why he is very close to God and God is very close to him. They understand each other perfectly. Such is the glory of the jñānī. He is ever aware, "I am not who I think I am. I am not this body, mind or intellect. I am Pure Consciousness. Pure Consciousness am I." This is the realization of a jñānī.

teṣhāṁ jñānī nitya-yukta
eka-bhaktir viśhiṣhyate I
priyo hi jñānino 'tyartham
ahaṁ sa cha mama priyaḥ II 7.17 II

****

Shloka 7.19

After many births of spiritual practice, one who is endowed with knowledge surrenders unto Me, knowing Me to be all that is. Such a great soul is indeed very rare

In his teachings Sri Shankaracharya says that we have to evolve through thousands of lifetimes before we become eligible for a human birth. After being born as a human being, it requires immense merit to come into contact with an enlightened Master. Without the guidance of a Sadguru it is impossible to understand the purpose of life or realize God. If we don't do this our whole life is wasted.

Who is a Sadguru? He is a great being who has performed *sādhana* for innumerable lifetimes in order to purify himself. Only when he attained this level of purity was it possible for him to realize the Lord in his heart. This is what the phrase *bahūnāṁ janmanām ante* in the shloka indicates. The phrase *vāsudevaḥ sarvam iti* is also extremely significant. The one who is in the hearts of all beings is Vāsudeva. To realize God in your heart is called the knowledge of Vāsudeva or Vāsudeva Jnāna. Once you realize that God is in your heart, you also realize that he is in the hearts of all living beings. This is called enlightenment. Such a person is very loving and compassionate because he sees the divine in everyone. That is what the phrase *vāsudevaḥ sarvam iti* means.

Very few beings have this realization. That is why it is so difficult to get a Sadguru. Until we get a Sadguru, we spend lifetimes in ignorance of our true nature. So we build up a lot of desires and karmic impressions or *samskāras*. As we keep taking one birth after another to fulfill these desires and exhaust our samskāras, fresh impressions are generated. We have already discussed how this creates a *kārmic* cycle and traps us in the web of *māya*. Sri Krishna is reminding us that in order to exit this cycle, we need the grace and guidance of a Sadguru which is a rare blessing that should not be taken for granted.

bahūnāṁ janmanām ante
jnānavān māṁ prapadyante |
vāsudevaḥ sarvam iti
sa mahātma su-durlabhaḥ || 7.19 ||

****

Shloka 7.25

I am not manifest to everyone, being veiled by My divine yoga māya energy. Hence, those without knowledge do not know that I am without birth and changeless

Sri Krishna said earlier that there are two types of nature: *parā prakriti* and *apara prakriti*, lower nature and higher nature respectively. The higher nature is consciousness, the lower nature is *sattva, rajo* and *tamo guna*; it's called *yoga māya,* which consists of the objective world, objective reality, objective experience. When people say they want to see God, they mean they want to experience God through the sense organs, the mind. Which means they are still attracted to *māya.*

God is beyond the sense organs and the mind, He is *nirākāra, nirguna.* But we are attracted to *saguna, sākāra* form. *yoga-māya-samāvṛitaḥ* - because of *yoga māya,* I am not available, 'I' being Sri Krishna Paramātma. You cannot experience the *nirākāra, nirguna chaitanya-swarūpi,* the nature of Consciousness. But it's available all the time! You are that Consciousness. By self-inquiry, you can always go back to your true nature which is *paramātma.* But people are attracted to objective reality. Objects, objects, objects. "I want to search for God!" Is God available in the temple? Is God available in the mountains? Is God available in some place? Then it becomes objective reality. Objective reality is nothing but Yoga māya.

A devotee of Krishna went to Ramana Maharshi. Because of his good Karma in his past life, he could play with Sri Krishna. When most children played with other children, he played with Krishna. Krishna was a living reality to him, available to the sense organs and the mind. He thought he was great. Sri Ramana Maharshi asked him: "Are you able to experience Krishna all the time? In your waking state, dream state and deep sleep state?". "No", said the devotee. Then he said "Find out what is available in all the three states. That's the real Krishna". So what is available to the sense organs and the mind is still *yoga māya*! That is why Ramakrishna Paramahamsa saw Mother Kali physically and interacted with her. All that was still in *yoga māya*. Then Totapuri told him, "Go beyond *yoga māya* and realize yourself, *ātma*, which is *nirākāra, nirguna*". Only then did Ramakrishna Paramahamsa go beyond that.

So the experience of God through the sense organs is called vision. It's good, no doubt it is good to have a vision of God, it will help in your purification. But still it's in *yoga māya*.

mūḍho 'yaṁ nābhijānāti loko mām ajam avyayam: Fools cannot understand me, fools meaning people who are ignorant. They cannot recognise me. *mām ajam avyayam* - I'm never born. *ātma* is never born. Consciousness is never born. And who is that Consciousness? You are that Consciousness! Find out the meaning of tat tvam asi, you'll realize this truth through *jnāna*.

nāhaṁ prakāśhaḥ sarvasya
yoga-māya-samāvṛitaḥ I
mūḍho 'yaṁ nābhijānāti
loko mām ajam avyayam II 7.25 II

****

Shloka 7.26

O Arjuna, I know of past, present, and future, and I also know all living beings; but Me no one knows

vedāhaṁ samatītāni - I know the past and present and future, Arjuna; *bhūtāni māṁ tu veda na kaścana* - but nobody knows me.

This wonderful universe, consisting of infinite stars, planets, galaxies, living beings, non living beings, there's a big, huge order in this universe; the order for creation, sustenance and destruction, the order for maintenance. The laws and rules are actually scientific principles or natural principles of life. One who has created this knows them all. He knows the past, present and future. He has all the knowledge of the past, present and future. But living beings cannot know him.

The only mechanism for knowing the Lord is the body, mind and intellect of living beings. But the body, mind and intellect cannot know the principle behind body, mind and intellect, the Consciousness. It is like this: what are the chances of a robot knowing the creator, a human being? A robot will never be able to know the creator, a human being. So all creations are creatures and the Lord is the Creator. It is very difficult for a creature to know the Lord, because the body, mind and intellect is only a vehicle. The body, mind and intellect cannot understand the Lord who is beyond sense organs.

But there is a possibility, a great possibility in the human being - the possibility of identifying himself not with body, mind and intellect but with the Creator, Consciousness. To understand 'I'm not the body, mind and intellect' and 'I Am Consciousness'. Then he has the ability to merge with the Creator. That's the only possibility. For all other living beings, it is impossible to know the Creator. It's like saying that a bulb knows electricity. A bulb will never be able to know electricity. But God has given a unique gift to human beings, to know themselves, to know the inner Self, which is nothing but God.

vedāhaṁ samatītāni
vartamānāni cārjuna I
bhaviṣyāṇi ca bhūtāni
māṁ tu veda na kaścana II 7.26 II

****

Shloka 7.27

O' descendant of Bharata, the dualities of desire and aversion arise from illusion. O' conqueror of enemies, all living beings in the material realm are deluded by these.

iccha-dvesa-samutthena - the duality born out of likes and dislikes, *iccha* and *dvesha*. *dvandva-mohena bhārata* - attached to this duality. *sarva-bhutani* - all living beings. *sarge yānti parantapa* - the moment they are born, they fall into *māya*.

Look at the beauty, the trap of *māya*. Immediately after being born from the mother's womb, you get into duality. The duality of like and dislike. Something hurts you, you start disliking. The child starts crying because it's back is hurting or it wants mother's milk. There's a liking for mother's milk and a dislike for hurt and pain. So dislike and like are the first dualities in life. So you get trapped in that duality, you get attached to that. The child starts getting attached to his like and dislike, the dualities. As it grows, the child accumulates more and more of these likes and dislikes. So the world is divided into what you like and what you don't like. This is the duality. What you like attracts your attention and it leaves a good impression on you. What you dislike you avoid, and it leaves a negative impression on you.

But both good and bad will drive you. Good impressions drive you to achieve more and more of that, while negative impressions drive you away from something unpleasant. These impressions are called Samskaras. They create tendencies called Vasanas. Vasanas create thoughts. Thoughts will create action. Action will create results. Result will create more impressions. It's a cycle. Slowly, slowly, you get into a cycle. You become a human being driven by more external conditions rather than conscious understanding of life. You get trapped in these external conditions. This is called 'dvandva'. This is by māya. It's very difficult to come out of this. And this starts right at the time of birth.

You need to come out of this unconscious cycle, this karmic cycle. You have to break this like-dislike cycle. You have to learn how to live with equanimity, only then can you come out of it. But it's very difficult for almost all human beings.

ichchhā-dveṣha-samutthena
dvandva-mohena bhārata I
sarva-bhūtāni sammohaṁ
sarge yānti parantapa II 7.27 II

****

Shloka 7.28

But persons, whose sins have been destroyed by engaging in pious activities, become free from the illusion of dualities. Such persons worship Me with determination

yeṣhāṁ tvanta-gataṁ pāpaṁ - Those who engage in good deeds and have good merits, those whose sins have reduced by *puṇya-karmaṇām* - meritorious deeds, *te dvandva-moha-nirmuktā* - they become free from the duality. And *bhajante māṁ dṛidha-vratāḥ* - they surrender to me, focus on me and with firm conviction, attain me.

There are people with divine qualities or *daivi sampat*, who constantly get involved in different kinds of spiritual activities which will purify them. Spiritual activities are of different kinds, different types, as

Bhagavān explained earlier: Karma Yoga, Bhakti Yoga, Jnāna Yoga and Kriya Yoga. These activities gradually purify oneself. What is the effect of purification? One whose mind is purified is freed from the duality, *dvandva*, likes and dislikes... I like this, I don't like this. He/she accepts any situation in life with equanimity. When you accept everything with equanimity, there are no further impressions created in your consciousness. Because there are no impressions created, there are no compulsive tendencies that will drive you towards external objects. So such a person's mind becomes pure.

Such a pure mind can get introverted, can turn inwards, to see the source of the mind which is the Lord Himself. That Source of the mind which is Consciousness. So the mind goes inwards, to find that Source. Such a mind has firm conviction, this conviction is not temporary, it does not waver. That conviction can come only after doing a lot of good merits. The mind has become pure. All the sins have gone. Sins are nothing but actions which are undertaken in ignorance. Those sins can dwindle by service oriented activities, by Yoga, activities related to Yoga. Such people become pure, their minds are focused inwards and they attain the Lord, who is the in-dweller of all living beings.

yeṣhāṁ tvanta-gataṁ pāpaṁ
janānāṁ puṇya-karmaṇām I
te dvandva-moha-nirmuktā
bhajante māṁ dṛiḍha-vratāḥ II 7.28 II

****

CHAPTER 8: AKSHARA BRAHMA YOGA

Shloka 8.5

Those who relinquish the body while remembering Me at the moment of death will come to Me. There is certainly no doubt about this

akshara means imperishable. *brahma* means Supreme Reality. The Yoga of that Supreme Reality which is imperishable is discussed in this chapter. We see everything in this world as perishable. A vegetable decays, rots in one week or four days and you have to throw it out. Your body itself is born, it grows, becomes old and dies. Everything is perishable, we don't see anything that is imperishable in the world. Nothing is permanent. We get attached to the objects of the world thinking that they are permanent in nature, right? They are not.

Everything in the world is impermanent. What about the world beyond? We think that after death, we go to some heaven or some place where we can have permanent happiness. Even that is impermanent. The scriptures, Vedas, say there are 14 lokas. They are called Bhuloka, Bhuvarloka, Svarloka, Maharloka, Janarloka, Tapoloka, Satyaloka, Atala, Vitala, Sutala, Talātala, Rasātala, Pātāla. So these are the lokas, higher and lower. Now these lokas are also perishable. So if you think that after death I will go to a higher planetary system where I can enjoy forever, that is also false. Even that is perishable. Brahma Loka lasts as long as Brahmaji is there. Even though the life of Brahmaji is a few thousand crores of years, he will also die and will attain liberation after death.

anta-kāle cha mām eva
smaran muktvā kalevaram I
yaḥ prayāti sa mad-bhāvaṁ
yāti nāstyatra sanśhayaḥ II 8.5 II

****

Shloka 8.6

Whatever one remembers upon giving up the body at the time of death, O son of Kunti, one attains that state, being always absorbed in such contemplation

yaṁ yaṁ vāpi smaran bhāvaṁ - that means whatever thoughts or feelings you have at the time of death, *tyajatyante kalevaram-* one who drops the body, *taṁ tam evaiti kaunteya* - he will attain that, the last thoughts that were there at the time of death, they will manifest. He will attain that body or that place which he was thinking at the time of death.

So there is a beautiful story in the Bhāgavata Purana about a King named Bharata. King Bharata, who was the ruler of India, went into meditation at the time of *vānaprastha*. After he completes his duties, he goes for *vānaprastha*, meaning he spends time in meditation for Self Realization. At that time, one deer gives birth to a baby and dies. Bharata starts taking care of the deer and as he becomes old, he constantly thinks of the deer. "Who will take care of this after I die?" was his last thought. In the next birth he is born as a deer.

Consider this - a very evolved person like Bharata also, at the time of death, had thoughts of a deer instead of God, and he takes that birth. What about common people? What about us? What kind of thoughts will we have at the time of death? Only those thoughts will manifest, right? That is why we should have the right kind of thoughts at the time of death. Bharata, after taking the birth as deer, remembers his past life because of his tapasya; because of his meditation practice, he conducts himself carefully even as a deer. In his next life he takes birth as a brahmin. In his next life he takes birth in a brahmin family and is called Jada Bharata; 'jada' means lazy. Jada Bharata appears to be lazy but in reality he was a realized soul at the time of birth. Because of his identification with the deer at the time of death, it takes him two lifetimes.

Therefore, says the Lord, be careful about what you think at the time of death. What you think at the time of death, is a summary of your lifestyle. Practise the right type of living, right thinking and you will have a beautiful death. And after that beautiful death, you will attain the Supreme Lord if you are thinking of the Supreme Lord at the time of death.

yaṁ yaṁ vāpi smaran bhāvaṁ
tyajatyante kalevaram I
taṁ tam evaiti kaunteya
sadā tad-bhāva-bhāvitaḥ II 8.6 II

****

Shloka 8.7

Therefore, always remember Me and also do your duty of fighting the war. With mind and intellect surrendered to Me, you will definitely attain Me; of this, there is no doubt

Next, we need to realize that unless we make it a habit of thinking about God during our lifetime, we will not be able to think about Him at the time of death!

Is that possible? As householders we need to work for our livelihood, we have families and careers to take care of. Where is the time to think of the Lord??

Bhagavān Himself gives a solution for this. Whatever you do and whenever you do something, think of Me, of Bhagavān. He tells Arjuna - while you're fighting the war think of me, because you don't know when death will come to you. This is the solution for all of us as well. Arjuna is fighting a war and death can come to him anytime, but us also death can come anytime. It will not give us an appointment. That's why we have to think of God all the time. Dedicate our life to God. Perform our duties as householders, professionals, but always think about God. If we can live with that attitude, life will be beautiful.

***tasmāt sarveṣhu kāleṣhu
mām anusmara yudhya cha I
mayyarpita-mano-buddhir mām
evaiṣhyasyasanśhayam II 8.7 II***

****

Shloka 8.14

O Partha, for those yogis who always think of Me with exclusive devotion, I am easily attainable because of their constant absorption in Me

ananya-chetāḥ - without thinking of anything else, *satataṁ yo māṁ smarati nityaśhaḥ* - one who thinks of me all the time, *tasyāhaṁ sulabhaḥ pārtha* - for such a yogi, it is easy to realize Me. *nitya-yuktasya yoginaḥ* means yogis who are engaged in activities and thoughts that are related to god.

We can constantly think of something which we like. If we like something, attracted to something, our mind will always be on that. So if we are attracted to God, then our mind will constantly dwell on God. The nature of mind is such that whatever it is attracted to, it stays on that.It is a natural process. You don't have to force it. You don't have to keep thinking, "No, I am not able to meditate on God". The moment we think of God and if other thoughts come in, it only means that our attraction to God is not strong enough.

One whose mind constantly dwells on God is called a Yogi. "For such a Yogi I am easily available" says Bhagavān. It is not difficult and attaining God is very easy for such a Yogi. *sulabhano hari sulabhano* sings saint Purandara Dasa in Kannada - it is very easy indeed to attain Hari. If we constantly think of Hari (lord), he will think of us. It is mutual. *tasyāhaṁ sulabhaḥ pārtha nitya-yuktasya yoginaḥ* - the Yogis think of God constantly, whatever their activities. Their mind doesn't waver, so He is accessible to them all the time. This is the promise of Bhagavān to his devotees - if you think of me , I will think of you!

ananya-chetāḥ satataṁ
yo māṁ smarati nityaśhaḥ
tasyāhaṁ sulabhaḥ pārtha
nitya-yuktasya yoginaḥ II 8.14 II

****

Shloka 8.15, 8.16

After attaining Me, the great souls, who are yogis in devotion, never return to this temporary world, which is full of miseries, because they have attained the highest perfection. (8.15)

From the highest planet in the material world down to the lowest, all are places of misery wherein repeated birth and death take place. But one who attains to My abode, O son of Kunti, never takes birth again. (8.16) mām upetya tu kounteya punar janma na vidyate - We keep on taking birth after birth, after birth, death and again birth and death. This cycle keeps on going. Why do we take birth, because we have pending desires to be fulfilled. The body is a vehicle for fulfilling our desires. So if with one body our desires are not fulfilled we take up another body. The cycle of birth and death thus continues. Till what point of time? Till you attain the lord, *mām upetya* - you have to attain the supreme reality, which is imperishable, beyond birth and death, such a supreme reality you have to attain.

It takes many, many lifetimes. Are these lifes easy? Every life is a hardship. So birth, growth, youth, old age, disease, death. Life is full of pain and suffering. It is not easy taking birth and undergoing death. So to escape this, the only route is to attain the supreme reality which is of the nature of bliss. Those who attain lord, those who think of lord, those who meditate on lord, contemplate on lord - they will attain the supreme reality, *sansiddhiṁ paramāṁ gatāḥ.*

Bhagavān says - *ābramha bhuvanālokāh punarāvartino arjuna.* The 14 lokas - Bhuloka, Bhuvarloka, Suvarloka, Maharloka, Janaloka, Satyaloka, Atala, Vitala, Sutala, Talātala, Rasātala and Pātāla - are also born, they stay for a while and they are destroyed. Nothing is permanent. *ābramha bhuvanāloka punarāvartinou* - so these lokas are perishable. These are not eternal. Nothing is eternal, everything is temporary. The lord alone, the supreme reality alone is permanent. So, ma *upetya tu kaunteya punarjanma na vidyate* - once you attain the lord, once you realize the lord in your heart, there will be no birth and death. You will be beyond birth and death. This is the promise lord gives.

mām upetya punar janma
duhkhālayam asāsvatam I
nāpnuvanti mahātmanāh
samsiddhim paramām gatah II 8.15 II

ābrahmabhuvanā lokāh
punarāvartino 'rjuna I
mām upetya tu kaunteya
punar janma na vidyate II 8.16 II

****

51

Shloka 8.24, 8.25

Those who know the Supreme Brahman pass away from the world during the influence of the fiery god, in the light, at an auspicious moment, during the fortnight of the moon and the six months when the sun travels in the north. (8.24)

The mystic who passes away from this world during the smoke, the night, the moonlight fortnight, or in the six months when the sun passes to the south, or who reaches the moon planet, again comes back (8.25)

Sri Krishna has mentioned in the earlier shlokas that whatever we think at the time of death we will attain that. Here, He is explaining what happens after death. These are the two shlokas where Sri Krishna explains the two paths - the Path of Light and the Path of Darkness.

Generally speaking, there are three paths for human beings. A person who realizes God in this lifetime is called a Jivanmukta, he is liberated. After death he does not go anywhere because he has attained the supreme reality of God in his current life. For him death can occur at whatever time or whichever place - it doesn't matter because he has attained the Supreme Reality. There is nothing pending for him.

Whereas for other people, there are two types of paths:

Path of Light - People who have worshiped God, who are devotees of Bhagavān - they will go on the 'Path of Light' - *uttarāyana mārga*. Fire and light are related to the internal wisdom or *jnāna*. Those who have the inner vision of inner reality or inner realization, they are on the path of light. Such people will go to a higher-level planetary system after death, to the loka of the deity they have been meditating on. They will attain that deity and will continue to stay in that loka. They will not come back to earth. This is called the 'Path of No Return' or 'Path of Light'.

Path of Darkness - On the other hand there is the 'Path of Darkness'. There are people who have done good deeds, but have not meditated on God. They have done good Karma or *punya karma*, what will happen to them? They will go on the *dakshināyana* or 'Path of Darkness'. Meaning, since they don't have the wisdom they will be on the path of darkness. They will go to heaven, where they enjoy the fruits of their actions. And after enjoying the reward for their good deeds, they will come back to earth. This is the path of return, the Path of Darkness.

So a person who has worshiped God but is not fully realized will take the Path of Light or path of no return. A person who has done good Karma will take the Path of Darkness, the path of return. An enlightened one who is alive, a Jivanmukta takes neither of these two paths. This is what Bhagavān tells us in these two verses.

agnir jyotir ahaḥ śhuklaḥ
ṣhaṇ-māsā uttarāyaṇam I
tatra prayātā gachchhanti
brahma brahma-vido janāḥ II 8.24 II

dhūmo rātris tathā kṛishṇaḥ
ṣhaṇ-māsā dakṣhiṇāyanam
tatra chāndramasaṁ jyotir
yogī prāpya nivartate II 8.25 II

****

Shloka 8.28

The Yogis, who know this secret, gain merit far beyond the fruits of Vedic rituals, the study of the Vedas, performance of sacrifices, austerities, and charities. Such yogis reach the Supreme Abode

Here Sri Krishna makes a clear distinction between the merit gained by performing Vedic rituals, studying the Vedas, austerity and charity and the outcome of constant meditation on the Lord. The *punya* or merit obtained in the first case takes us to heaven after death. But when the merit we have accumulated is exhausted, we are reborn on earth. Therefore we are still trapped in the *karmic* cycle of repeated births.

This is not so in the case of a seeker who immerses himself in constant thought of the Lord. God or consciousness is eternal in nature. So when we meditate on consciousness, we are established in the Self forever. This is not temporary. It cannot be reversed. We realize our true nature and abide there permanently. We are liberated from the cycle of repeated births.

vēdēṣu yajñēṣu tapaḥsu caiva
dānēṣu yatpuṇyaphalaṅ pradiṣṭam I
atyēti tatsarvamidaṅ viditvā yōgī
paraṅ sthānamupaiti cādyam II 8.28 II

****

CHAPTER 9: RĀJA VIDYĀ RAJA GUHYA YOGA

Shloka 9.2

This knowledge is the king of sciences and the most profound of all secrets. It purifies those who hear it. It is directly realizable, in accordance with dharma, easy to practice, and everlasting in effect

Welcome to the 9th chapter of Bhagavad Gita, in which the Lord teaches us Rāja Vidya, Rāja Guhya, royal path of knowledge or royal secret. *pavitram* - it is very, very purified and *idam uttamam* - it is the greatest knowledge; *pratyakṣhāvagamaṁ dharmyaṁ* - it is the real dharma, *su-sukhaṁ* - it is joyful, *kartum avyayam* - and is easy to follow

So this is the type of knowledge I am going to give you (says Krishna). What is that knowledge? Rāja Vidya means knowledge of the Lord directly given by the Lord. One who doesn't have understanding of the Lord cannot give this knowledge. When Bhagavān tells about himself, it is direct knowledge and he also gives the path of attaining Him. That is why it's the royal knowledge, the royal path.

Why is royal knowledge a royal secret? Because royal secrets are not known to the public - only the king and royal family will know, right? Royal secrets are closely guarded secrets. Similarly, not everybody knows about the Lord; it's a royal secret. The Lord will reveal it only to true devotees. And what is that secret? It is about the Lord himself - What is He all about? How is He the entire universe? Those who listen to these secrets will get purified, says Bhagavān.

rāja-vidyā rāja-guhyaṁ
pavitram idam uttamam I
pratyakṣhāvagamaṁ dharmyaṁ
su-sukhaṁ kartum avyayam II 9.2 II

****

Shloka 9.4

This entire cosmic manifestation is pervaded by Me in My unmanifest form. All living beings dwell in Me, but I do not dwell in them

mat-sthāni sarva-bhūtāni - all living beings are in me, but I am not in them. This is very puzzling - every living being is in the Lord, but the Lord is not in the living being! The Lord is *avyakta*, unmanifest, He is beyond birth and death. All living beings are subject to birth and death, is it not? The Lord pervades the entire creation as pure Awareness. In that sense everything is in Awareness. For example the wall you see in a room is in Awareness, the table is in Awareness, the chair is in Awareness. Whatever picture comes into Awareness is *jada* or insentient. The jada is seen in the light of Consciousness. You see the chair because of the light of Consciousness - so that chair is in Awareness. I see the bed because of the light of Consciousness. The bed is in Awareness.

What about the body and mind? They are also seen in Awareness. So the entire world is in Awareness. But is there Awareness in the chair? Is there Awareness in the wall? They are insentient. There is no sentience in them. *jada* or *prakriti* is dependent on *chetana*. The entire manifestation is in the Consciousness, but Consciousness is not in the manifestation because it is *jada*. But, you may say, I (as body) appear to be alive. That body, mind and intellect is also glowing in the light of Awareness. The Awareness reflected in the body and mind gives life. But body and mind in itself are *jada*. The body and mind are in Awareness, but Awareness is not in them.

The primary reality is *chetana* - Awareness or Consciousness. *jada* or insentience is the secondary reality or dependent reality. The Lord is declaring this truth.

maya tatamidaṅ sarvaṅ
jagadavyaktamūrtinā I
matsthāni sarvabhūtāni
na cāhaṅ tēṣvavasthitaḥ II 9.4 II

****

Shloka 9.10

Working under My direction, this material energy brings into being all animate and inanimate forms, O son of Kunti. For this reason, the material world undergoes the changes (of creation, maintenance, and dissolution)

mayādhyakṣheṇa prakṛitiḥ sūyate sa-charācharam - Bhagavān is saying that the whole universe, which is called *prakriti* or nature, runs under the rulership of the Lord.

prakriti consists of millions of stars, planets, galaxies; the entire universe is insentient - *jada*. It is not sentient, but it appears to be so. There is motion, there is movement, there is friction, there is action, there is intelligence in the universe. For example, at the right time the sun rises and sets, from time to time the seasons change, plants grow. In nature, everything is happening spontaneously. Nature appears to be intelligent, but the intelligence is coming from the Lord, Consciousness. Nature is a dependent reality, Consciousness is an independent reality. The Lord is Consciousness, and in this light of Consciousness all of nature, *prakriti* operates. Consciousness is not the doer, it's the non-doer, it's that Consciousness which runs the universe.

It's like the sun because of which plants grow, animals live, the seasons change, every change on earth happens. Without sunlight, there is no movement, nothing happens on the earth. But the sun is not the doer. It is the cause, but the sun by itself does nothing. So, the Lord is the master, and under Him the Universe operates.

mayādhyakṣheṇa prakṛitiḥ
sūyate sa-charācharam I
hetunānena kaunteya
jagad viparivartate II 9.10 II

****

Shloka 9.11

When I descend in My personal form, deluded persons are unable to recognize Me. They do not know the divinity of My personality, as the Supreme Lord of all beings

avajānanti māṁ mūḍhā - they are fools, who don't know the God, don't know Bhagavān. Why? *mānuṣhīṁ tanum āsritam* - because they are identified themselves with the human body. *paraṁ bhāvam ajānanto mama bhūta-maheśhvaram* - I'm the God of all beings, living beings. Such people can't understand my supreme nature, because they are identified with the body-mind complex.

So, to understand God is two ways:

God is in the heart of all living beings. He is in your heart, he is in my heart, he is in the heart of a dog, he is in the heart of a monkey. But we don't know that. If I ask you, "Who are you?", you'll say, "I'm a human being, I'm a man, I'm a woman". You identify yourself with the body, but you ignore the *ātma*, which is the Self. The body by itself has no life or no Consciousness. It is the *ātma* which gives Consciousness to the body. Without *ātma* you are nothing, you are nobody. The *ātma* is the God of the body, but you don't identify with that because you don't know that the *atma* exists. You identify with the body, which means, you don't know that God is in your heart. You are ignoring the God in your heart, who is the master of the body-mind complex.

There is another way of knowing this truth. God will take *avatāra* or incarnate on earth whenever there are disturbances on a massive scale. During such times, to uphold Dharma, God takes up a form. But even then people will not be able to recognize Him because they identify themselves with the body. God too, with all His glory and power, is mistaken for a body. Bhagavān calls them fools. We have to realize that we are not the body, mind or intellect, but pure Consciousness. Recognize the God within us and in all living beings. Recognize God as an Avatāra Purusha.

avajānanti māṁ mūḍhā
mānuṣhīṁ tanum āsritam I
paraṁ bhāvam ajānanto mama
bhūta-maheśhvaram II 9.11 II

****

Shloka 9.12

Bewildered by the material energy, such persons embrace demoniac and atheistic views. In that deluded state, their hopes for welfare are in vain, their fruitive actions are wasted, and their culture of knowledge is baffled

Useless desires, useless actions and useless knowledge - these are the characteristics of fools (*avivékis*). They are said to have a demoniac nature. What is meant by useless or fruitless action?

People have desire, so, what is this desire for? The desire is to get happiness, find peace and to achieve that we do a lot of things. However, searching for happiness and peace in the world is fruitless. We do experience happiness sometimes but the next moment it slips away, and all over again we try something else to get happiness. And it goes on.

For example, people go to the racecourse with a bag full of cash to bet on horses. They get excited when the horse is winning and start getting depressed when it loses. Then come back empty handed. What are these people doing over here? What is anybody doing? They are chasing happiness. They are trying to purchase happiness. The pursuit of happiness is valid, but it is in the wrong direction. Because of wrong knowledge, they think that happiness lies in the objects. Happiness is not in the objects, whereas it is within them. It is in their inner-self. If the understanding is wrong, actions will also be wrong. As their thinking is wrong, they acquire demoniac nature because they go to any extent to attain that.

moghāśhā mogha-karmāṇo
mogha-jñānā vichetasaḥ I
rākṣhasīm āsurīṁ chaiva
prakṛitiṁ mohinīṁ Sritāḥ II 9.12 II

****

Shloka 9.13

O son of Pritha, those who are not deluded, the great souls, are under the protection of the divine nature. They are fully engaged in devotional service because they know Me as the Supreme Personality of Godhead, original and inexhaustible.

mahātmanas tu māṁ pārtha – O' Arjuna, *daivīṁ prakṛitim āsritāḥ* - people with the divine qualities, *bhajantyananya-manaso* - continuously worship me; *jñātvā bhūtādim avyayam* - knowing that, I am the cause of all the living beings

64

This is a very interesting shloka. God is the cause of all living beings. He is *avyayam* - immutable or unchangeable. All living beings are born in Him, He is the cause.

Whenever a person says I come from my father and mother, he refers to the biological father and biological mother, isn't it? The biological father and biological mother are responsible for our birth, but we never trace back our source to God.

It can be explained in this manner - what are we? We are nothing but a body-mind-intellect combination, plus Consciousness. The body-mind-intellect is coming from the five elements of nature - earth, water, fire, air and space. Consciousness comes from the Bhagavān.

So, who are we really coming from? We are coming from God, we are children of the divine. But we forget this and connect with our biological parents. They do have a role because they have given birth and have taken care of us, but the source of our life is God, Consciousness is God. The body-mind is *prakriti* or nature. In other words, we are directly related to the universal father and the universal mother.

tvameva mata pita tvameva - you are the mother. Who is our mother? It is *prakriti* or nature. But nature has no independent existence, it is functioning because of Consciousness. So who is the father? Consciousness is the father. *tvameva bandhu sakhā tvameva, tvameva vidyā dravinam tvameva* - if we analyze in this manner, we are directly related and connected to God in every way. We could be connected through friends or relatives. God alone is our father, God alone is our mother, God alone is our relative and God alone is our friend, God alone is our guru. This is what Bhagavān is emphasizing here.

Not everybody can understand this; only people with *daivi prakriti* or divine qualities can understand this. Such people with divine qualities who can understand this are called *mahātma* or great souls. Because they are able to understand this, they think of Me all the time, says Krishna. Whenever they see their father or mother they think of God. Also, when they see their friends or relatives they think of God because they are in relationship with God and not with the body and mind.

mahātmanas tu māṁ pārtha
daivīṁ prakṛitim āsritāḥ I
bhajantyananya-manaso
jñātvā bhūtādim avyayam II 9.13 II

****

Shloka 9.14

Always chanting My glories, endeavoring with great determination, bowing down before Me, these great souls perpetually worship Me with devotion.

satataṁ kīrtayanto - those who constantly think of me, *māṁ yatantaśh cha dṛiḍha-vratāḥ* - those who are focussed on realizing god, constantly do *namaskara* or prostration to God. Such *mahātmas* constantly think of me and they constantly worship me. *satataṁ kīrtayanto* - to always think of God, always praise God. This is the teaching.

mahātmas are great beings or great souls. They understand the glory of God and they realize the nature of God as the all-pervading reality. They realize that God is in all living beings. Whatever they see or whatever experience they grasp, they remember God. *kirtana* means to sing songs. It need not be only singing songs of praise; it is to live in constant gratitude and remembrance of God. It is like doing *namaskara*; not only physical *namaskara* but also to live in an attitude of surrender to God.

dṛiḍha-vratāḥ - their mind doesn't get deviated because their mind is focused on God. There are many people who do some worship, and forget it.

There are many people who try to do puja and forget it. If worship is done like a temporary activity, the mind cannot be focussed. But the devotees whose mind is focussed on God do it constantly.

nitya-yuktā upāsate - such people do it all the time. They live in the attitude that everything is the glory of God; everything is divine. Everywhere they see God, deep inside. Such beings are great beings.

satataṁ kīrtayanto māṁ
yatantaśh cha dṛiḍha-vratāḥ l
namasyantaśh cha māṁ
bhaktyā nitya-yuktā upāsate ll 9.14 ll

****

Shloka 9.22

But those who worship Me with devotion, meditating on My transcendental form- to them I carry what they lack and preserve what they have

ananyāśh chintayanto māṁ ye janāḥ paryupāsate - there are devotees who constantly think of God without diverting their attention. That is called ananya. God says, I will take care of *yoga* and *kshema* of such devotees.

One should understand the words *yoga* and *kshema*. *yoga* means to get something that you do not have, *kshema* means protecting what you already have. Here, God says that he will make sure that you will get what you don't have and he will also protect what you already have.

For *yoga*: Those devotees who are constantly thinking of God, want God only. They need nothing else other than God. God alone is the reality. So, God will make sure that they get that. Hence, they realize God. That is called *yoga*.

For *kshema*: *kshema* means that God will protect that wisdom of the devotee. It's not that they will realize today and forget it by tomorrow. He will take care of realization and that experience continuously.

yoga-kṣhemaṁ vahāmyaham - I shall take care of such devotees, says Bhagavān. Whom does God take care of? Those who are constantly thinking of God, those who are seeking God, those who are seeking Godly experience for themselves. I will take care of such devotees. This is *yoga-kshemam* in the spiritual sense.

yoga-kshemam has a material sense also. If somebody is involved in devotional activities and he is facing some difficulties in his life, then God will take care of him. How?

Once there was a poor Brahmin who was working on the teachings of Bhagavad Gita. He had read the meaning of this shloka *yoga-kṣhemaṁ vahāmyaham* as God will take care of yoga and kshema. But then while writing he thought, it could mean that God will send somebody to take care. So, he wrote down the translation as 'God will send somebody to take care of his devotees'. It so happened that due to some financial difficulties, there was no food in his house. When the Brahmin had gone out for some work, there came a little boy named Gopal with a basket full of food items and gave them to his wife, saying "your husband has sent this." and disappeared.

After the Brahmin came home the wife thanked him for the food items. Confused, the Brahmin said, "No! I didn't send anybody. Who gave you this?" "A little boy named Gopala" said the wife (Gopala is another name of Krishna). Amazed, the brahmin went back to his study and looked again at the changes he had made - 'God himself will take care' to 'God will send somebody to take care'. He understood now that he had blundered- he changed the sentence back to 'God himself will take care'. This is the teaching of Bhagavad Gita. God protects you, takes care of you.

Here is another story of Akbar and Birbal. Akbar also asked Birbal, why would God come himself to take care of any devotee? Birbal said, "Yes Lord, I can prove it." One day, Akbar and Birbal were walking near a lake where the king's son was boating. Even as they were looking, the boat overturned and the little prince fell into the water. Without thinking twice Akbar jumped into the water to rescue his son.

Later he realized that it was not his son who fell into the water but a doll made out of wax to resemble his son. Angry, Akbar demanded, "What kind of prank is this Birbal?" Birbal replied, "O' King, why did you jump into the lake yourself? You could have called some servants to do so" Akbar responded, "It's my son who was drowning- I couldn't have wasted any time in calling someone else!" "Exactly," said Birbal, " being an emperor, you jumped into the water to save your son. Likewise, God, the Emperor of the Universe, will jump and save the devotee when needed." This is the message of this verse.

ananyāśh chintayanto māṁ
ye janāḥ paryupāsate I
teṣhāṁ nityābhiyuktānāṁ
yoga-kṣhemaṁ vahāmyaham II 9.22 II

****

Shloka 9.25

Those who worship the demigods will take birth among the demigods; those who worship ghosts and spirits will take birth among such beings; those who worship ancestors go to the ancestors; and those who worship Me will live with Me.

People worship different things in life. Some worship different deities or demigods. Some people worship ghosts. Some people worship ancestors. Some people worship the Supreme reality, the God or Bhagavān. Whatever you worship, you get that.

To understand this you can think of a government structure. It has a Prime Minister, IAS officers, and police officers and many more roles in the government. For somebody who doesn't know the government structure, the ordinary police constable itself becomes the entire government. He goes and does namaskaram to the police constable to get his work done. Whereas, someone who knows the Prime Minister will interact with him directly. So, it depends on what you see as the larger picture.

The universe is formed by God. There are also demigods or devatas who rule the universe, comparable to IAS officers in a government structure. Many people worship them. For example, there is a demigod responsible for rain. So some worship the Rain demigod for blessings. Those who worship such demigods ultimately reach the loka of that demigod after death. There are some people who think, "Oh, What is more important to me are my ancestors." Gods are not important because my survival depends on my ancestors. They worship ancestors and they go to *pitru loka*. There are other people who are more interested in worshiping various kinds of demons. Such people will reach the world of demons.

Depending on what you worship, you attain that, says Bhagavān.

yānti deva-vratā devān
pitṝn yānti pitṛi-vratāḥ I
bhūtāni yānti bhūtejyā
yānti mad-yājino 'pi mām II 9.25 II

****

Shloka 9.26

If one offers Me with love and devotion a leaf, a flower, fruit or water, I will accept it

patraṁ puṣhpaṁ phalaṁ toyaṁ - people offer different things to God. Rich people offer gold ornaments.

Super rich people may build temples. They may offer so many things to God depending on their capability. But, is God looking for what you can afford to give?

Once when I went to a temple somebody remarked, "That person is a great devotee of God". I asked, "How do you know he is a great devotee? What makes him a great devotee?" He said, "Because he donated a gold necklace weighing 1 kilo to the deity in that temple." So according to that logic, if someone gives 1 kilo of gold, then he becomes a great devotee. And if someone else gives two kilos of gold, he becomes a greater devotee. People have this kind of concept in their minds.

Bhagavān says, "It is not what people give Me, it is with what attitude they give it to Me that matters." You need not offer expensive items to God. Even if you offer some *phalam* - fruit, *patram* - leaf, *pushpam* - flower, and *toyam* - water, with a pure heart, with loving heart, He will accept it with love.

God is looking for your heart. God is looking for what you offer with love, not what items you offer. He is looking for your attitude, your inner Consciousness. "That I will accept" God declares.

patraṁ puṣhpaṁ phalaṁ toyaṁ
yo me bhaktyā prayachchhati I
tadahaṁ bhaktyupahṛitam
aśhnāmi prayatātmanaḥ II 9.26 II

****

Shloka 9.27

O' son of Kunti, all that you do, all that you eat, all that you offer and give away, as well as all austerities that you may perform, should be done as an offering unto Me

yat karoṣhi - whatever you do, *yad aśhnāsi* - whatever you eat, *yaj juhoṣhi* - whatever you offer in the worship of player, *dadāsi yat* - whatever you donate, *yat tapasyasi* - whatever austerities you do, all that you offer that to Me says Bhagavān. In other words, whatever actions you perform, you do it as a devotional service.

For our living we have to perform so many activities. When we perform these activities, we have to pray, "O God, whatever actions I am doing, let them be done for your service. Whatever fruits/whatever result you give, I will accept it as prasadam." If you perform actions in that manner, your life will be beautiful.

Everything done as a dedicated service to God is devotional service.

There was a saint named Kabir Das. He was a Muslim but a great devotee of Lord Rama. Once somebody asked him, "O' Kabir Das! You chant Rama's name all the time. Because you are a muslim, obviously, you won't be allowed to enter the temple of Rama. Even your fellow men will not allow you to mosque because you are chanting a hindu God's name. Then how will you worship?" Kabir Das said, "Where I go, it becomes *pradakshina* for God. Whatever I eat becomes *naivedya* for God. Whatever I see becomes an offering to God. I live my life with that attitude and don't do anything specific. All activities of my life are devotional service to God."

In this story, God indicates how you can convert every action of yours into a devotional service.

yat karoṣhi yad aśhnāsi
yaj juhoṣhi dadāsi yat I
yat tapasyasi kaunteya
tat kuruṣhva mad-arpaṇam II 9.27 II

****

Shloka 9.29

I am equally disposed to all living beings; I am neither inimical nor partial to anyone. But the devotees who worship Me with love reside in Me and I reside in them.

samo 'haṁ sarva-bhūteṣhu - I am present in all living beings in equal proportions; *na me dveṣhyo 'sti na priyaḥ* - I have neither enmity towards anyone nor is anyone close to me. I'm present in all living beings. But those who are devoted to me, they are always in Me and I am always in them.

This statement appears to be a bit strange. The Lord or Bhagavān is present in all living beings in equal proportions. Be it an ant or an elephant, dinosaur or whale or a human being, Consciousness is present in equal proportions. It is not that somebody has more Consciousness and somebody has less Consciousness. But the human body-mind complex can reflect Consciousness to a greater extent. Just like the sun - the sun shines equally on all objects but it is reflected more in water but less in stone. Similarly, the Lord is present in all living beings in equal proportions, He is the Consciousness in them. He has neither enemies nor friends. He is the *sakshi* or the witness in all.

Bhagavān however goes on to say that, those who are devoted to me 'they are in me' and 'I am in them'. The phrase 'they are in me' is easy to understand, because all living beings are in the Lord. But here when He says 'I am in them', He implies that the quality of reflection of the divinity will be higher in His devotees. This is because they constantly think of Bhagavān.

samo 'haṁ sarva-bhūteṣhu
na me dveṣhyo 'sti na priyaḥ I
ye bhajanti tu māṁ bhaktyā
mayi te teṣhu chāpyaham II 9.29 II

****

Shloka 9.30

Even if the vilest sinners worship Me with exclusive devotion, they are to be considered righteous because they have made the proper resolve

Even a sinner who continuously meditates on Me should be considered as a saint, because his intellect has become focussed and purified. So, a sinner might commit a sin as per the laws of the world. Thanks to some opportunity or God's grace, he may start opening up to divine qualities by uttering God's name. Then he may start worshiping God, focussing on God. Then gradually an inner transformation happens within him. Gradually he becomes a better person and later, a saint.

Most of us are familiar with the story of how a hunter called Ratnakara became the great poet Valmiki. Ratnakara the hunter lived in the forest, killing unfortunate passers-by to loot their money. One day Sage Narada visits him and asks, "You are committing a crime and acquiring a lot of sin! Why are you doing this?"

Ratnakara says, "It is for taking care of my family." Narada retorts, "will your family members partake of your sins as well?"

So Ratnakara rushes to his wife and asks her the same question. "No, I won't take any share of your sins", says the wife. The children also refuse to do so. Ratnakara comes back to Narada and confesses that none of his family members was ready to share his sins. "What should I do now?" asks Ratnakara. "Stop sinning and chant the name of the Lord!" advises Sage Narada, and teaches him to chant the *rāma-nāma*.

Ratnakara was a hardcore criminal. By chanting *rāma-nāma*, he becomes purified. His mind becomes very pure. He goes on to write beautiful poetry called the Rāmāyana, and comes to be known as Vālmiki. Vālmiki is called the *ādi kavi* or the ancient poet who wrote the entire Rāmāyana in lyrical verses. So that is the glory of chanting God's name. This is the glory of meditating on Bhagavān - even sinners turn into saints.

There are other examples in the modern times. Srila Prabhupāda went to America. He stood in Times Square and was chanting Hare Krishna Hare Krishna. A lot of hippies who were wandering gathered around him. The US government was spending a lot of money on rehabilitating drug addicts, in vain. These hippies started chanting the name of Hare Krishna along with Prabhupāda, and soon they got transformed. Many of them got purified and became great saints. All by chanting the name of the God, this is the glory of chanting.

There is of course another popular story of Buddha and Angulimāla. Buddha was going through a forest inhabited by a thief called Angulimāla. He used to kill people who passed through the forest, take their thumbs and make it into a garland and wear it. When Buddha walked towards Angulimāla, he was very impressed by Buddha's poise - he did not display any fear. This was enough - Angulimāla became Buddha's disciple. In no time he went on to become one of the arihanta - an enlightened one.

This is the glory of chanting God's name.

api chet su-durāchāro bhajate
mām ananya-bhāk sādhur
eva sa mantavyaḥ samyag
vyavasito hi saḥ II 9.30 II

****

Shloka 9.32

All those who take refuge in Me, whatever their birth, race, gender, or caste, even those whom society scorns, will attain the supreme destination

For Bhagavān, all are equal. He has no distinction of upper caste, lower caste or gender. There is no high and low. For a mother who has five children, all are equal to her. Similarly for the Lord, everybody is equal. All are his children.

But some of us in the world do not have equal opportunities because of societal conditions. In earlier days, probably post Vedic period for example, women, business class and the lower caste had less opportunities for spiritual education. Lack of spiritual education obviously is a problem - for such people, progress in spiritually is difficult. But there is an easier way to attain the Lord- all one has to do is to surrender to the Lord, chant the Lord's name. All will be uplifted. This is what the Lord says here. He doesn't look at your education, he doesn't look at how much you have. But he looks at what you are. Even people who lack spiritual education and opportunities to acquire it also can attain the Lord.

māṁ hi pārtha vyapāsritya
ye 'pi syuḥ pāpa-yonayaḥ I
striyo vaiśhyās tathā śhūdrās
te 'pi yānti parāṁ gatim II 9.32 II

****

Shloka 9.34

Always think of Me, be devoted to Me, worship Me, and offer obeisance to Me. Having dedicated your mind and body to Me, you will certainly come to Me

Many of us put in a lot of effort to attain our goals in life. For instance, an athlete desirous of participating in the Olympics practices for over ten years. He works day in and day out with complete focus. If we want to attain God, we must dedicate our mental space only to him and nothing else.

Our mind should be completely focussed on him in deep adoration. Every thought, word and deed is an offering to him. Our body is a chariot for the Lord and our mind is his sanctum sanctorum. When we live like this, our mind becomes extremely pure. Then it becomes possible to attain God. This is the promise given to us by Sri Krishna.

man-manā bhava mad-bhakto
mad-yājī māṁ namaskuru I
mām evaiṣhyasi yuktvaivam
ātmanaṁ mat-parāyaṇaḥ II 9.34 II

****

CHAPTER 10: VIBHŪTI YOGA

Shloka 10.8

I am the source of all creation. Everything originates from Me. The wise who know this perfectly, worship Me with great faith and devotion

We see many things happening in the world. Everything that happens has a cause and effect. When we try to analyze these causes and effects, we may find that it stretches into an endless chain. Instead we could also ask, "This vast creation must be created and sustained by some powerful force. What is behind this cosmos? What is the cause behind all causes?"

Sri Krishna says that the cause of all causes is God. It is from him that everything comes. This incredible cosmos has been created by him. If we ask scientists about how the world began, they say that it began with a Big Bang. If we persist in the enquiry and ask, "What was there before the Big Bang?" they have no answer. But the scriptures tell us that God is the powering energy behind the universe.

God not only creates, he also sustains. The cosmos around us is so complex. There are millions of galaxies and innumerable stars and planets in each galaxy. All of them move in their own orbits. Obviously, there are laws governing everything in the universe to maintain this meticulous order. There are also many forces like the gravitational, centrifugal and centripetal forces. All of them work together to preserve the balance of the cosmos. If these laws collapse, this entire creation will collapse. It is the Lord who ensures that the universe functions with perfect synchronicity. This is possible because the cosmos arises from him, exists in him and dissolves into him. jnānis or enlightened beings understand this great truth.

Let us approach this from another direction. Where do we come from? We reply, "That's easy. We came from our parents of course." All right, where did our parents come from?" Well, from their parents, right? This can go on endlessly. Yes, we certainly got our bodies from our parents. But this body is made up of five elements – earth, water, fire, air and space. These were generated by the energy in Nature. Who gave us consciousness? God. So though we trace our origin to our biological parents, our real parents are consciousness and energy.

aham sarvasya prabhavo
mattaḥ sarvaṁ pravartate I
iti matvā bhajante māṁ
budhā bhāva-samanvitāḥ II 10.8 II

****

Shloka 10.9

With their minds fixed on Me and their lives surrendered to Me, My devotees remain ever content in Me. They derive great satisfaction and bliss in enlightening one another about Me and in conversing about My glories

If we like cricket, we spend hours watching and playing cricket. If we find the stock market interesting, we keep checking whether the market trends and share values are rising or falling. If we enjoy trekking, we spend a lot of our time on treks. We always focus on what we find attractive or interesting. When we are engaged in doing what we like, we are happy and time flies by.

Similarly, devotees of God find great joy in thinking of him. Their thoughts, feelings and energy flow only towards God. Their love for God draws them together. They extol his glory and describe his greatness to each other. God's qualities inspire them and give them confidence. They spend their time in devotional service. This is the nature of the devotees of the Lord.

mach-chittā mad-gata-prāṇā
bodhayantaḥ parasparam I
kathayantaśh cha māṁ nityaṁ
tuṣhyanti cha ramanti cha II 10.9 II

****

Shloka 10.10

To those whose minds are always united with Me in loving devotion, I give buddhi yoga by which they can attain Me

When we serve God constantly and immerse the mind in devotion, he is pleased with us. Intense focus on God also removes unnecessary thoughts and purifies the mind. When the mind is pure and subtle, we are eligible for Jnāna or Buddhi Yoga. Out of compassion, God ensures that we receive this knowledge when we are ready for it.

What is Buddhi Yoga? It is the understanding that we are one with the Lord. *tat tvam asi* or You are That is the teaching of the Upanishads. You are not separate from God. This conviction and clarity liberates us from the wrong belief – I am the body. Buddhi Yoga is the result of devotional service we offer to the Lord.

teṣhāṁ satata-yuktānāṁ
bhajatāṁ prīti-pūrvakam
dadāmi buddhi-yogaṁ
taṁ yena mām upayānti te || 10.10 ||

****

Shloka 10.11

Out of compassion for devotees, I, who dwell within their hearts, destroy the darkness born of ignorance, with the luminous lamp of knowledge

Though God is always in the heart, we ignore Him. We are not aware of his presence in us or in anyone around us. This is called ignorance. Ignorance is of two types - *āvarana* and *vikshepa*. *āvarana* is the veil which makes us forget that we are one with the Self or *paramātma*. When we forget our true nature, the body and world are projected because of *vikshepa*. Acting synchronously, *āvarana* and *vikshepa* create the illusion that I am the body. To shatter this illusion, God manifests in the intellect. Then the wisdom, 'I am not the body, mind and intellect. I am Pure Consciousness' dawns in the intellect.

If we want to become Self-aware, God's grace is indispensable.

teṣhām evānukampārtham
aham ajnāna-jaṁ tamaḥ I
nāśhayāmyātma-bhāva-stho
jnāna-dīpena bhāsvatā II 10.11 II

****

Shlokas 10.12, 10.13

Arjuna said: You are the Supreme Divine Personality, the Supreme Abode, the Supreme Purifier, the Eternal God, the Primal Being, the Unborn, and the Greatest. The great sages, like Narada, Asita, Devala and Vyasa proclaimed this, and now You are declaring it to me Yourself

paraṁ brahma paraṁ dhāma - brahman is supreme reality; *pavitraṁ paramaṁ bhavān* - you are the purest; *puruṣhaṁ śhāśhvataṁ* - you are the supreme being; *divyam ādi-devam ajaṁ vibhum* - you are light, the primal being, unborn, great.

Parabrahman, the Lord is the Supreme Reality, the formless reality. His place or the abode is *parama dhāma* or the supreme abode. We stay in a house, but when we go out of the city we stay in a hotel or guest house, but we feel uncomfortable in a hotel and once we return to our house, we get comfortable.

Even that house, what we call our house, is not really our house. If it's a rented house we have to change the house since it is not ours. Then, there is a house called body, we live in the body, but the body is also not a permanent house. After we die, we have to leave that body and move to another body. Thus there's nothing called a permanent house here on earth, but there is something called the eternal abode - *parama dhāma*, the abode of the Lord. We can reach the abode of Lord, *parama dhāma*, the resting place which is our true nature. Our true nature is called *parama dhāma*.

The Lord is of the nature of *sat chit ananda* i.e. Truth, Consciousness, Bliss. Consciousness is pure and Consciousness is the eternal subject. Everything in manifest reality appears in Consciousness, and whatever appears in Consciousness has birth and death. The world appears in Consciousness. This world has birth and death. The body appears in Consciousness and so this body has birth and death.

The body has lots of impurities; it has blood vessels, has pus formation, passing of body fluids etc. Everything is a part of the body. But the *atma* who is residing in the body is pure. It is of the nature of Consciousness. The *atma* is one with the *paramatma*, the Supreme Reality, so it is pure. The Lord is eternal, everything else has a birth and death. Everything created in the world has birth and death, but Bhagavān doesn't have birth and death. *divyam adi-devam*, He is pure, He is light.

What light is this? This is not the physical light, it is the light of Awareness. He is the *ādi deva* - the beginning of everything. So, creation happened billions of years ago. Who was there before creation? Consciousness, the Lord, *adi-devam ajam*, and from Him, the universe came into existence.

Then, there are the devatas who rule us, the different beings, entities who manage the universe, all of them came from the Lord. Hence, He is the *ādi deva*. He is vibhum, the master of this universe, He controls this universe. Who says so? All the realized beings like Devarshi Narada, Asita Rishi, Devala Rishi, Vyasa Rishi, all the Rishis sing His praise. And now, Bhagavān HImself is declaring this truth to Arjuna! Rishis are second in line of the information, they teach what they know, but the Lord is telling Arjuna directly!

arjuna uvācha,
paraṁ brahma paraṁ dhāma
pavitraṁ paramaṁ bhavān I
puruṣhaṁ śhāśhvataṁ divyam
ādi-devam ajaṁ vibhum II 10.12 II

āhus tvām ṛishayaḥ sarve
devarṣhir nāradas tathā I
asito devalo vyāsaḥ
svayaṁ chaiva bravīṣhi me II 10.13 II

****

Shloka 10.41

Whatever you see as beautiful, glorious, or powerful, know it to spring from but a spark of My splendor

Each one of us is different and there are different objects. Creation has lots of variety and beauty. There are many aspects of creation like mountains, valleys, rivers, forests, birds, animals etc. Everything is wonderful in this creation - so much of variety and so much of beauty. The Lord says look at this creation - whatever you think is beautiful, wonderful and glorious, know that it is all my glory. They all come from a small part of my divine light.

Look at Lord's marketing technology. We are familiar with product marketing, right? The marketing salesman will say - look at this product, these are the features, this is how the product looks and performs... he makes the product interesting to you. Then you try it or buy the product.

The Lord says the entire universe is my creation. It is like an art gallery, so many beautiful paintings, wonderful paintings are there, they all are lovely. You look at the paintings, and wonder at its beauty, wow, what a painting! You see another painting and are struck by its beauty. You wonder about the painter, you ask, who is the painter? Similarly, the Universe is nothing but a painting of the Lord. It is a sculpture of the Lord. The whole purpose of it all is to give you the creation, to attract your mind and make you curious to know the Creator, the Consciousness behind it, to go back to Consciousness. This is the way of the Lord to attract you back to him.

yad yad vibhūtimat sattvaṁ ś
hrīmad ūrjitam eva vā I
tat tad evāvagachchha tvaṁ
mama tejo 'nśha-sambhavam II 10.41 II

****

Chapter 11: VISHVARŪPA DARSHANA YOGA

SUMMARY

Arjuna prayed to Sri Krishna and said, "O' Lord please show me your divine form." Krishna appeared before him in his cosmic form. Arjuna saw the seven netherworlds – Atala, Vitala, Sutala, Talātala, Rasātala, Mahātala and Pātāla. He also saw the seven higher planes Bhuloka, Bhuvarloka, Suvarloka, Maharloka, Janarloka, Tapoloka and Satyaloka. There were many kinds of beings inhabiting each plane of existence – human beings or *manavas, gandharvas, kinnaras, kimpurushas, devas and asuras.*

The vision encompassed the past, present and future. All the beings who existed in the past, who are in the present and who will exist in the future were part of the Lord's Cosmic Form. That is why the Vishnu Sahasranama or the 1000 names of Lord Vishnu begins with the phrase *vishwam vishnur vashatkāro* which means that the Lord is present in every atom of the universe. He is the core of sentient and insentient aspects of creation. He is the past, present and future. He is time and space.

Arjuna witnessed worlds being created, sustained and destroyed. He beheld bewitching beauty and terrifying phenomena. Galaxies, stars, planets and heavenly bodies appeared and disappeared. He saw the horror of destruction on a cosmic scale – worlds getting smashed, burning to ashes and merging into Consciousness. He saw kings and warriors being killed in the Mahabharata war he was yet to fight. Now, we must remember that Arjuna was no novice to the battlefield. He was a great warrior. He had fought many wars and killed thousands in combat. He had seen all the horrors of warfare at close quarters.

Yet he was now overwhelmed and petrified by the Cosmic Form that Sri Krishna revealed to him. Shivering uncontrollably and covering his eyes he cried, "Enough, Krishna, enough. Please revert to your beautiful form. I cannot bear this terrifying vision any longer." So Sri Krishna assumed the smiling form of Narayana with his conch, mace and disc. This chapter reveals that God is present in every atom of creation. It highlights the truth that everything happens according to his divine plan.

****

Shloka 11.54

O Arjuna, through single minded devotion alone can I be known as I am, standing before you. Thereby, on receiving My divine vision, O scorcher of foes, one can enter into union with Me

You should have a single minded focus to realize God. What is single minded focus? When we want to achieve something, we have to focus our minds on it and work hard. Whether it is getting good scores in an exam or winning a race, we should concentrate on it without getting diverted. That should be our first priority and everything else should be secondary. If this is the kind of focus we need to achieve the ordinary goals of life, then imagine how much greater it has to be to realize God.

Sri Krishna says that knowledge is of three types - *jñātuṁ draṣhṭuṁ cha tattvena praveṣhṭuṁ cha. jñātuṁ* means acquiring a comprehensive knowledge about your goal. Who is God? What are His qualities? What is His true nature? We have to listen to the glories of God that the Puranas and Upanishads describe. The person who extols God should speak with conviction and clarity. Then his fire of knowledge will ignite a blaze in us. Rather than reading a scripture, if we listen to a Jnāni explain it, his words touch us deeply and transform us.

Srimad Bhāgavatam, the scripture that narrates the story of Sri Krishna says that if we want to understand his glory, the best way is to see him through the eyes of the milkmaids or Gopikās of Vrindavan. They thought and spoke only about Lord Krishna all day long. They adored him single mindedly. Applying the dust of the Gopikās' feet to our heads will give us a true understanding of Sri Krishna, says the Bhāgavatam. To symbolize this we apply the yellow paste of Gopi Chandana to our foreheads during worship. If we have the focus of the Gopikas, then we are sure to realize God. To acquire the knowledge of God or jñātuṁ is the first step on the journey.

The second step, *draṣhṭuṁ*, is seeing God. How can we have a vision of God? Sri Ramakrishna Paramahamsa sang the praises of Goddess Kali. Day and night he thought only of his divine mother. So he started having visions of Mother Kali. He could see her and talk to her. He fed her and received prasadam from her hands. Mother Kali was a living, breathing entity for Sri Ramakrishna. Yes, if we have intense devotion, we can see and experience God in the form of our favorite deity. But the problem with this is that it is temporary. The vision appears and disappears and we have very little control over it. Moreover, we know that God is infinite. But in a divine vision we are confining infinity with our mind and sense organs. We are limiting God to just one form when he is simultaneously present in all beings. There are two types of experiences – anubhava and anubhūti. In anubhava we experience something through the mind and sense organs. anubhūti is direct knowledge without the intervention of the mind and senses. This is permanent and ultimate.

.

This is the third step of merging permanently with the principle called God - *tattvena praveṣhṭuṁ*. It is irreversible. For Sri Ramakrishna this happened when his Guru Totapuri came. Totapuri said, "Goddess Kali is a vision. Though she seems very real to you, she is merely an appearance. She is part of the māya that binds you. Go beyond her. Transcend the form of Mother Kali and realize God as your own Self." Sri Ramakrishna did as he was bid and became established in the Self. This is called aparoksha anubhūti or direct knowledge.

Sri Ramakrishna explains *anubhūti* through a parable. A salt doll walked into the ocean to measure its depth. Can you tell me what happened to that salt doll? Yes, it dissolved completely in the ocean. The doll was gone and only the ocean was left. This is what is meant by merging with the principle called God. The one who sees through your eyes, hears through your ears, smells through your nose, tastes through your tongue and feels through your skin is

God, Bhagavān. God is the eternal witness. He powers our senses and mind. Without his power nothing works. But we egotistically think that we do everything. No, it is the Lord. So you have to offer yourself to God like the salt doll that dissolved in the ocean.

To sum up, single pointed focus means listening to the glories of God from a Jnāni, having a vision of God and then realizing God as your true nature. These three steps need not necessarily happen in this order. The question is, do we have this kind of focus or is our mind getting diverted here and there? Sri Krishna promises that when we have intense devotion and unwavering focus, we will realize God.

bhaktyā tu ananyayā śhakya
aham evaṁ-vidho arjuna I
jñātuṁ draṣhṭuṁ cha tattvena
praveṣhṭuṁ cha parantapa II 11.54 II

****

Shloka 11.55

Those who perform all their duties for My sake, who depend upon Me and are devoted to Me, who are free from attachment, and are without

malice toward all beings, such devotees certainly come to Me

When we discussed *nishkāmakarma*, we understood that when we perform each task as an offering to God and accept the result as his grace or *prasāda*, life is free from fear and stress. A seeker who lives in this way is always very clear that the only goal in his life is to realize God. He loves God so much that he is attached to nothing else.

We are attached to so many things in life. We keep saying, "I want this, I want that." A devotee of the Lord says, "What will I do with all these things? The happiness they bring me is gone in a few moments. I want nothing but my Lord." He hates nobody. He has no enmity with any living being because he sees Bhagavān in all of them. His heart overflows with love and compassion for all beings. Sri Krishna says, "When a devotee is so focused and devoted, he will certainly attain Me." These are the qualities required for realizing God.

mat-karma-kṛin mat-paramo
mad-bhaktaḥ saṅga-varjitaḥ I
nirvairaḥ sarva-bhūteṣhu yaḥ
sa mām eti pāṇḍava II 11.55 II

****

CHAPTER 12: BHAKTI YOGA

Shloka 12.5

For those whose minds are attached to the unmanifest, impersonal feature of the Supreme, advancement is very troublesome. To make progress in that discipline is always difficult for those who are embodied

There are two ways to realize God - through form and the formless. Human beings are embodied souls with a very strong identification with the body. Because of this it becomes very difficult to visualize the formless aspect of God.

For most of the human beings to cultivate devotion for God is much easier when associated with a form. That's the message.

kleśho 'dhikataras teṣhām
avyaktāsakta-chetasām I
avyaktā hi gatir duḥkhaṁ
dehavadbhir avāpyate II 12.5 II

****

Shloka 12.8

Just fix your mind upon Me, the Supreme Personality of Godhead, and engage all your intelligence in Me. Thus, you will live in Me always, without a doubt.

Bhagavān explains here as to how one should have devotion. The mind and intellect both should focus on God. The mind is the outer part, the intellect is the inner part. Mind is the one which sees the world, the mind is the one which interacts with the world and experiences the world. Mind is called *manas*. Whereas intellect is called *buddhi*. Intellect makes judgment, discriminates and guides, it is the inner part.

So, our dedication should be such that the manas and buddhi should be completely focused on God. So, it's not that you just have your mind focussed on God but intellect is not focussed. The nature of intellect is such that it will throw a lot of questions.
"Oh! is this Lord?"
"Is he available?"
"Can I really meet him?"

This is the *buddhi. manas* says "I want to see God". Mind is trying to experience God. But *buddhi* says, "Oh! Is there something really called God? Where is he?"

Or there could be a case where *buddhi* has become clear that "I have to see God". But *manas* will not stay still. Mind would want to think of God then a thought of a sweet might occur. Mind might again want to think of God and again another thought of watching a movie might occur. So, the mind will keep changing.

So, *buddhi* and *manas*; the inner and outer part of our consciousness has to be aligned and focused on God.

mayy eva mana ādhatsva
mayi buddhiṁ niveśhaya I
nivasiṣhyasi mayy eva ata
ūrdhvaṁ na sanśhayaḥ II 12.8 II

****

Shloka 12.9

My dear Arjuna, O winner of wealth, if you cannot fix your mind upon Me without deviation, then follow the regulated principles of bhakti-yoga. In this way you will develop a desire to attain to Me

If you are not able to focus your mind on God, then try to do repeated effort/practice. By this you will reach him.

In earlier shlokas, God had told that if you want to attain Bhagavān, you have to focus your mind on him. Perform devotional services for God. But for some people it is not possible, because they have a flickering mind. Mind is like a monkey - jumps here and there. What to do in such cases? God says not to worry, there is a solution for this too. Practice is the solution. By repeated practice you'll be able to focus your mind. By focusing your mind, you will be able to attain me.

You can compare this with learning to cycle. Initially you will keep falling often while learning to ride a bicycle. To balance on two wheels is not easy. You may need somebody else's support. When you start riding, you may fall again. But if you keep practicing, one day you'll be able to ride the bicycle without anybody's support.

Similarly, if you keep on practicing devotional service and hence focussing the mind on God, you'll not fall. You'll attain Me eventually, says God.

atha chittaṁ samādhātuṁ
na śhaknoṣhi mayi sthiram I
abhyāsa-yogena tato mām
ichchhāptuṁ dhananjaya II 12.9 II

****

Shloka 12.10

If you cannot practice the regulations of bhakti-yoga, then just try to work for Me, because by working for Me you will come to the perfect stage.

Earlier Sri Krishna told Arjuna to focus his mind on Him constantly. If he was not able to focus his mind, then practice doing so, said the Lord. Now if he is not able to do that either, what to do?

Then God says there is another way. Do service – do devotional service. Do all the work as an offering to the God i.e., devotional service to the God. When you do that, you are working for God, and He is in your mind all the time. Meditation or focusing the mind inwards requires some amount of mastery of the mind. Mind has to go inwards. For most of us it may not be possible because the mind is focussed outwards. In such cases doing any work is easier. Devotional service is easier. God says if you are not able to take your mind inwards and focus on me then do devotional service or Karma Yoga. Consider everything as an offering to God. And whatever fruits come – good or bad, accept it as a prasadam or gift from God. Then in this process you'll become purified. Because of the purification, you can focus your mind and concentrate on God.

abhyāse 'py asamartho 'si
mat-karma-paramo bhava I
mad-artham api karmāṇi
kurvan siddhim avāpsyasi II 12.10 II

****

Om Sadguru Devaya Namaha

PURCHASE DETAILS

(Scan QR codes to visit these links)

Book Purchase: https://notionpress.com/author/592662

CONTACT DETAILS

(Scan QR codes to visit these links)

Website: www.lightoftheself.org

Programs from Light of the SELF Foundation

1. **Atma Darshana** - Journey of Self discovery

2. **Jnāna Jyothi** - Study Advaita Vedanta

3. **Gita Jyoti** - Study Bhagavad Gita

4. **Yuva Jyoti** - iLeader Youth Leadership Program

5. **Bhakti Jyoti** - Learn Veda Mantras and Bhajans

6. **Yoga Jyoti** - Learn Yoga

Email id : lightofself@gmail.com